THE *Re*FASHION HANDBOOK

Refit, Redesign, Remake for Every Body

BETH HUNTINGTON

stashBOOKS.

an imprint of C&T Publishing

Text and Photography copyright © 2014 by Beth Huntington

Photography and Artwork copyright © 2014 by C&T Publishing, Inc.

Publisher: Amy Marson

Creative Director: Gailen Runge

Art Director/Book Designer:
Kristy Zacharias

Editor: Liz Aneloski

Technical Editors: Alison M. Schmidt and
Mary E. Flynn

Production Coordinator: Jenny Davis

Production Editor: Katie Van Amburg

Illustrator: Jenny Davis

Photo Assistant: Mary Peyton Peppo

Styled photography by Nissa Brehmer,
unless otherwise noted; Before and
instructional photography by Beth
Huntington, unless otherwise noted

Published by Stash Books, an imprint of C&T Publishing, Inc., P.O. Box 1456,
Lafayette, CA 94549

Library of Congress Cataloging-in-Publication Data

Huntington, Beth, 1960-

The Refashion handbook : refit, redesign, remake for every body / Beth Huntington.

pages cm

ISBN 978-1-60705-923-3 (soft cover)

1. Clothing and dress--Remaking. 2. Clothing and dress--Alteration. I. Title.

TT550.H86 2014

646.2--dc23

2014003195

Printed in China

10 9 8 7 6 5 4 3 2 1

Dedication

To my mom, Katharine Crichton, who taught me to keep my enthusiasm for life, no matter what, and to always move forward to experience joy and new beginnings.

Acknowledgments

There are so many people who encouraged me along the way, and I'd like to thank a few of them.

Thank you to the editors, Roxane Cerda, Liz Aneloski, and Alison Schmidt; the photographers, Diane Pedersen and Nissa Brehmer; and the art director, Kristy Zacharias, at Stash Books, who had so much patience with me and magically made this book into something even better than I ever dreamed.

Thank you to my family for putting up with the photo/sewing studio that overtook our entire house all summer and for going without all the home-cooked meals I usually fix for you, so I could fulfill this dream. Thank you for believing in me and encouraging me every step of the way.

Thank you to Jan, Karin, and Katie for sending out all those good thoughts into the universe and being there for me.

I want to thank my couture seamstress friend, Linda, who inspires me to be a better seamstress, makes me laugh, and helps me find clarity when I become stuck in quagmires of ideas.

Thank you to my friend Kris, one of the most generous people I know. The Renegade Seamstress blog and this book became realities because she gave me her old Digital Rebel XT and Photoshop Elements 6, and tutored me all along the way.

Finally, I want to thank my mom and my sister, who cheered me on from heaven, who guided my hands, my words, and my heart the entire time I was writing this book. I felt their spirit beside me the whole way on this book-writing adventure.

Contents

THE *Re*Fashion HANDBOOK

Introduction

There's a reason I'm called The Renegade Seamstress. Could it be because I'm a maverick refashioning outlaw ready to rid the world of fashion mistakes? Perhaps! Could it be because I'm wild and creative, I'm really fun to hang out with, and you just might learn some sewing skills from me? Perhaps! Could it be because I don't always do things the conventional way? Perhaps!

No matter what I call myself, I just want you to know that if I can do this, anyone can! I have no formal sewing training. My training consists of Mrs. Kunze's home ec class in high school and what my mom passed on to me. Much of what I know is self-taught through experimentation, trial, and error. To me, that's half the fun of creating: going through the process of learning by doing.

I don't profess to know all the correct methods of sewing, and I'm sure there are books out there for those of you who would like to become couture seamstresses. This book isn't intended to be a sewing bible, by any means. This book is, however, a collection of techniques that have allowed me to give some pretty bad thrift store clothes a whole new life. I want to show you some basic skills that will help you to get started in this fantastic world of refashioning. I want to inspire you with project ideas.

It is my hope that after reading this book, you will never look at thrift store clothes the same way again. I hope that after you try creating some things on your own, your mind will be flooded with the endless possibilities of re-creating something beautiful and modern from "past-their-prime" items. I hope you will redefine your fashion by creating your own clothes. I hope this will become your new hobby.

Really, it's true; if I can do this, anyone can! So channel the Renegade Seamstress that lives deep within you, grab your scissors, fire up your sewing machine, and let's get started.

Redefine Fashion,
ONE *Re*FASHION AT A TIME

In the past few years, there's been an exciting resurgence in the sewing world. It could be because of Pinterest. It could be because of the countless online sewing communities bringing these creative people together. It could be the popularity of *Project Runway*. It could be a new awareness of the cost of fast fashion. Or it could be because we've all had to tighten our belts (so to speak) in the last few years. Whatever the reason, it's fun to see young men and women taking on this creative new hobby and fun to see people who haven't sewn for years dust off their sewing machines and take up a needle and thread again.

Refashioning isn't a new thing. It's actually been around for a long time. During World War II, when clothes rationing was introduced in Great Britain, there was a movement called Make Do and Mend. The Ministry of Information published a pamphlet outlining the ways to make your clothes last longer. For many people around the world with limited shopping opportunities, refashioning has always been a way of life. If you're concerned about your impact on the environment, refashioning instead of buying new can reduce your carbon footprint considerably.

Reconstructing clothing can also be a very economical way to build a wardrobe for work and play. Sometimes all it takes is a quick trip to the thrift store to find something inexpensive to refit, redesign, or remake. You could even reconstruct some outdated items from your own closet, which costs nothing! Jackpot! I know I'm fortunate to have my local thrift shop. Most days, all items of clothing are a dollar. On Wednesdays, adult clothing is only 50 cents. There never seems to be a shortage of clothes with possibilities. But even if you don't live close to a thrift shop as good as mine, there are still crazy good deals to be had on tired-out clothing items that just need someone with some vision to come and rescue them.

I started to refashion so I could have clothes that fit me perfectly. I was tired of standing in a mall dressing room, looking in the mirror and thinking there was something terribly wrong with my body just because the clothes didn't fit. I was tired of spending my hard-earned money on clothes that would never fit properly. I was tired of promising myself I'd do more sit-ups and eat more salads, just so I would fit into clothes that obviously weren't made for my body. When I learned to refashion used clothing, not only did it cut down considerably on my clothing budget, but I ended up with clothes that actually fit my body perfectly, and I had fun making them in the process.

Another great reason to refashion is that quite often a pattern isn't necessary. Commercial patterns can be expensive, and when you combine that outlay with the cost of fabric, zippers, buttons, and thread, making clothes from scratch can become more expensive than buying them. In addition to being pricey, commercial patterns still need to be altered to fit your body. If you're not well versed in the fitting aspect of patterns, all of your hard work and money might be wasted on an ill-fitting final garment.

Another beauty of refashioning is the idea that half the work is done for you already. I quite often use the existing zippers, buttons and buttonholes, collars, sleeves, and hems. This cuts down on loads of work and can be a money saver, too.

Whatever your reason for refashioning—being kind to the earth, saving money, getting the perfect fit, or not using a pattern—to me, the best reason to refashion is the fun you'll have doing it. Redefining your fashion is a great way to make your wardrobe your very own. Each piece you reconstruct will be your own design. No need to be concerned about someone else wearing the same outfit when you've created it yourself.

YOU MIGHT JUST
Surprise Yourself

If you walk into my kindergarten classroom on any given day, you will most likely hear a sweet little five-year-old voice happily proclaiming, "Hey, Mrs. Huntington, I just surprised myself!"

This one declaration alone makes all my hard work as a teacher worth the effort. I love the look of pure joy on the children's faces when they accomplish what they set out to do. I love seeing them develop confidence by trying new things. I love watching them develop the skills they need to become successful. When the going gets tough and they think they can't do it, I reassure them by reminding them that if they just try, they might just surprise themselves.

This is exactly what I want to tell you, too. It is my hope that this book will give you the tools to be confident and successful in your refashioning adventures and will inspire you to try your hand at redefining your fashion. I just know if you jump in and give it a try, you will surprise yourself. If you've wanted to do this but didn't know where to start, then this is the book for you.

Many people tell me they think you need to be an excellent seamstress before you can start to refashion. Actually, nothing could be further from the truth. Sure, you need a few basic tools and skills. But that's what I'm here for. Sure, you need to be able to solve some problems once in a while and make it up as you go along. But really, that's half of the fun, don't you think? Sure, you need to be able to look at an old garment and see the new life within it, but that just takes practice. The feeling of creative license, of taking what you know about something and running with it, is so exhilarating. To jump in with both feet and try something new is so rewarding.

Sometimes people tell me they are afraid to make a mistake. You know what I say to that? Mistakes, smishtakes. Who cares! If it doesn't turn out, it's OK; just set it aside and try something else. With every mistake comes learning. With every mistake comes growth. With every mistake comes new opportunity. I say go for it. Just start cutting and the rest will follow. If you're shopping at thrift stores, you most likely aren't spending much moolah on your items to refashion, so who cares if something doesn't turn out. You just have to be willing to take that risk, jump in with both feet, and not let fear of mistakes stop you from trying this. Joseph Chilton Pearce says, "To live a creative life, we must lose our fear of being wrong." How right he is!

I truly believe, armed with a few basic sewing skills and this book to help you get started, you will be well on your way to creating your own perfectly fitted wardrobe from cast-off clothing for a fraction of the price you'd pay for something new.

SECRETS TO
Thrift Store Shopping

About ten years ago, I decided to cut back my hours at work so I could spend more time at home with my family. It was during this time I learned to appreciate shopping at thrift stores. It was a blessing to be able to find things I needed for very little money. I want to share with you some of the secrets to shopping at thrift stores that I have learned along the way.

Even though I'm back to work full time now and I don't have to pinch pennies as much as I used to, I still spend lots of time in thrift shops. They're really some of my favorite places to shop. When some people think of thrift store shopping, they start to panic and imagine smelly, dark, and depressing places. But really, nothing could be further from the truth. Most thrift stores are well organized, bright, and full of friendly people and treasures. One of my favorite quotes comes from motivational speaker and author Wayne Dyer: "When you change the way you look at things, the things you look at change." This is the very first secret to thrift store shopping. Instead of looking at the clothes as tired, old, and worn out, look at them as raw materials, possibilities of new beginnings, hope for the future. Perhaps the sweater is stretched out and has some holes.

Could you use an intact part of it for boot socks or a tote bag? Could you remake it into something new? Perhaps the style is outdated. Could you cut it apart and use the fun fabric to make it more modern? Could you redesign it? Perhaps it's huge. Could you alter it to fit you perfectly? Could you resize it? Truly, once you start to look at thrift store clothes this way, you will realize the endless possibilities waiting for you each time you step through the door of a thrift shop.

In addition to seeing the possibilities of each garment, you'll need to train your eye to look for interesting details, quality fabrics, and great patterns. This is the second secret to thrift store shopping. When you train your eye, thrift store shopping can become an adventurous treasure hunt. I don't always know immediately what I'm going to make, but many times I'm drawn to something on the garment and, if the price is right, I'll buy it and put it in my stash for later. It's all about seeing things with new eyes—whether it's our relationships, our situation, our home, our job, or even our old clothes. When we adjust our vision, or what we focus on, that's when the magic happens.

The third secret for successful thrift store shopping trips is to look for the sales. In order to keep their merchandise moving and fresh, most thrift stores will have a half-price day. Usually a certain color tag is on sale. Some thrift stores will have monthly bag sales. Usually you will pay a set price for a bag full of items. Some thrift stores will even give you a discount if you bring in a bag of clothes to donate. Donating some clothes back to the store is also a good way to keep your stash from overtaking your home. When I thrift shop, I usually look at the sale items first. I don't

like to spend much money on items to refashion. It makes me much more likely to take risks and start cutting if I know I didn't spend much on a piece of clothing.

Another secret to thrift store shopping, especially if you love to refashion as much as I do, is to look in unexpected places. Check all the sizes. Don't limit yourself to your regular size. I'm an average size, and sometimes my section doesn't have much. The larger-size clothing will give you plenty of material to work with and you can find some great fabrics and styles. Just a few modifications can result in some great changes. The too-small section might even reveal garments with great usable fabrics or some that could be altered to fit. The children's section and the men's section can also hold some amazing treasures for you. I once found a huge, beautiful, soft, unworn cashmere sweater tucked in the back of the men's section and bought it for a song. It became one of my favorite peplum sweaters. Finally, don't forget about the linen section. This section is filled with sheets, tablecloths, curtains, blankets, and pillowcases. Quite often, you'll find some with quality fabric that can be made into wonderful clothes. I was lucky enough to score a vintage Vera tablecloth and vintage Vera sheets in this section and made some fun outfits from these collectible old linens.

I hope you feel that, armed with these shopping secrets, you can confidently grab your purse and head for the nearest Goodwill, Savers, or Salvation Army and be on the lookout for that perfect sweater to remake, that perfect dress to redesign, or that perfect shirt to refit. Hey, we might even be waving to each other over the men's shirt rack.

ORGANIZE
Your Space

If you love to refashion and sew as much as I do—
and I know once you start, you will—you'll want to
create an organized storage area so you can find
what you need at a moment's notice. There is nothing
worse than being hit with inspiration and having to
spend your creative time searching for just the right
piece of fabric or the perfect garment to use in your
project.

When I started out reconstructing clothing, my local thrift shop was having a canned food drive. In exchange for four cans of food, you would get a garbage bag to fill with whatever your heart desired. Whoa, my kitchen cupboards became empty as I kept perusing the racks and envisioning what each and every one of those sad garments could become. I felt like I was rescuing them from the dump or someone's rag pile. It almost became my civic duty to give them all a new life. Some people rescue dogs; I guess at that time my mission became apparel rescue.

After washing each and every item, I folded them all neatly on my kitchen table and marveled. I first bought two large plastic tubs at the thrift store to store everything. Little did I know that those tubs would soon be overflowing and I'd have to come up with a better way to organize. In comes my ruggedly handsome contractor husband to the rescue. Using scraps of wood and a small area on my back laundry porch, he lovingly made a double closet rod for me to hang all my soon-to-be-refashioned clothes. Oh, it was so pretty with everything hanging there, all color coordinated, with easy access to everything I needed. When inspiration hit, there was just no stopping me. Well, as time passed and I made trips to more and more thrift shops, I even started to grow out of this system. I found a tall shelf unit at the Salvation Army and added that to the back porch. I folded all my treasures so nicely and placed them, again by color, on each shelf. Sometimes I would just gaze upon all this possibility and dream for enough time to create all the masterpieces that kept flowing through my brain.

Just a friendly word of warning, though: With all of the inexpensive thrift store clothes that have refashioning potential, there is a very real possibility that your home will become overrun with your stash. Don't be afraid to purge once in a while to keep your stash fresh. If you've had an item for a long time and it just keeps getting shoved to the back, send it back out into the world. There might just be a budding seamstress who needs that particular item to create her vision. If your stash gets too overloaded and cumbersome, your creative ideas can't flow the way they should.

Whatever organizational strategy you decide to use, make sure it's easily accessible, neat, and inspirational when you look at it. Your creative mind and your family will thank you!

ESSENTIAL TOOLS
for Refashioning

When you reconstruct clothes, you will need just a few simple tools to get started.

SCISSORS are one of your most important tools. If you can have only one pair, invest in good all-steel scissors. Keep them as sharp as possible. If need be, hide them from your family so they are never used on paper, pipe cleaners, pop cans, or anything else. No kidding—that actually happened in my house. I've almost even gone as far as putting a padlock on the handles when I'm not using them. You probably won't have to go that far, but they need to stay sharp!

The SEAM RIPPER will be your new best friend. I actually have many of these handy "best friends" strewn about on almost every table and by nearly every chair in my house. Choose one you like because it'll be in your hands quite often.

Make sure you have a quality IRON. Purchase a heavy one with a stainless steel plate and a good steam function. I have this weird thing about ironing: I love it! There is something so soothing about ironing out the wrinkles and making everything smooth and neat. Keeping your fabric and seams smooth will ultimately result in a beautifully made garment.

Your MEASURING TAPE will actually become your sewing necklace. Keep it around your neck and handy at all times.

MARKING CHALK or a WASHABLE FABRIC MARKER is a "must have" item when you are refashioning. It's good to have several different colors and types of marking tools so the marks will show up on different types and colors of fabrics. Make sure to test that the marks can be removed on the different fabrics and garments you work with.

You will use good sharp PINS on practically every project. I keep mine in the flower-shaped plastic box they came in, but lately I've had my eye on some super-cute handmade pincushions. As a matter of fact, I was secretly coveting the bright, fun pincushion my friend Jakki made for Elizabeth's bridal shower. Maybe someday … (hint, hint).

Another important tool is your sewing machine NEEDLE. You'll need several different sizes and types. Each fabric calls for a different needle. If you notice your stitches going wonky, it is most likely because the needle isn't right for the particular fabric you're using (see Know Your Needles, page 22). You'll also need a variety pack of hand-sewing needles in different sizes.

And finally, you'll need a SEWING MACHINE. It doesn't have to be a fancy one. Mine is a very basic Singer machine, and it has served me well for many years. I am often asked if I use a special machine to refashion. Sure, a serger would be nice, but for now, all you really need is a basic machine to accomplish all the projects in this book.

If you're planning on making bags or quilts, a ROTARY CUTTER, RULERS, and CUTTING MAT come in handy for making precise cuts. I love my rotary cutter and use it all the time.

A DRESS FORM is nice but optional. I do use mine quite often, but even though I can set it to my exact measurements, it's not the same shape as my body. I still have to try on my garments several times as I'm making them to ensure proper fit.

Armed with this book and these tools, you should be able to refashion anything your heart desires.

BASIC
*Re*Fashioning
SKILLS

Measuring for Fit

In order to complete a successful refashion, you'll need several measurements. So gather up a friend you can trust, a flexible measuring tape, a pencil, and a sewing notebook. The measurements I use most often are my waist, hips, distance from waist to hips, bust, arm circumference, arm length, distance from waist to preferred hem length, and distance from shoulder to waistline. There are many other measurements you'll need if you decide to get into pattern drafting, but for now, these are the basic measurements you'll need.

After taking each measurement, record it in a notebook that you keep handy in your sewing space.

Use the measurement chart (on the following page) to record your measurements.

TO MEASURE YOUR BUST, raise your arms to shoulder height and have your friend place the tape across the widest part of your breasts, under your arms, and around your back to where you started. Make sure to keep the tape level across the back.

FOR YOUR WAIST MEASUREMENT, wrap the measuring tape around your natural waist (this is usually the smallest point, not necessarily where you wear your waistband).

TO MEASURE YOUR HIPS, wrap the measuring tape around the largest part of your hips.

TO MEASURE THE DISTANCE FROM YOUR WAIST TO YOUR HIPS, place the end of the measuring tape on your natural waistline, at the side, and measure straight down to the largest part of your hips.

FOR YOUR UPPER ARM CIRCUMFERENCE, measure around your bicep.

TO MEASURE YOUR ARM LENGTH, bend your arm slightly at the elbow, start at your shoulder (feel for the bony point), and measure down the outside of your arm and over the elbow to your wristbone.

TO MEASURE THE DISTANCE FROM YOUR SHOULDER TO YOUR WAIST, hold the beginning of the tape on the top of your shoulder, run it down over your bust, and have your friend read the tape at your waistline.

TO DETERMINE THE DISTANCE FROM YOUR WAIST TO YOUR DESIRED HEM LENGTH, hold the beginning of the tape at your natural waistline and let the tape fall straight down your side. Have your friend read the tape at your desired hem length. You might want to measure several skirt lengths at once.

Now take these measurements, grab a pair of scissors, and fire up your sewing machine. You should be able to tackle almost any refashioning project your heart desires.

MEASUREMENT CHART

Bust

Waist

Hips

Distance from waist to hips

Arm circumference

Arm length

Distance from shoulder to waist

Distance from waist to desired hem length

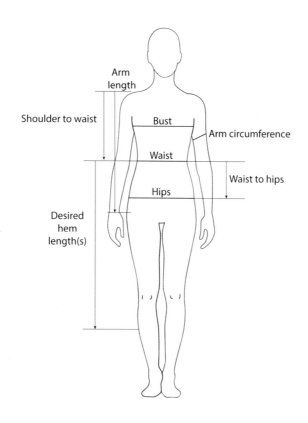

Arm
length

Shoulder to waist

Bust

Arm circumference

Waist

Waist to hips

Hips

Desired
hem
length(s)

Know Your Needles

The type of needle you use can sometimes be just as important as the fabric you choose. If you're encountering stitch difficulties, nine times out of ten it'll be a simple fix: Just change your needle. Even as I was writing this book, when it came time to demonstrate different types of stitches, my tension was off and I was trying all the different tensions on my machine, consulting my machine manual, and even consulting Google for how to adjust bobbin tension. Then, all of a sudden I had a facepalm moment—of course! I had just been working with silk, and I had a silk needle in my machine. That needle isn't going to work on thick denim. Hence the importance of using the correct needle when sewing on different fabrics.

	Silks/Sheers	Cotton/Quilting	Medium Weight	Denim/Canvas	Leather/Layers of Denim
NEEDLE SIZE	70/10	80/12	90/14	100/16	110/18

You will also need to be aware of what type of needle you are using. There are universal needles, which are for wovens, but you'll also need to have ball-point or jersey needles, made for knit fabrics. In addition to universal and ball-point, you may need a leather needle. Leather needles have a chisel point to help make a hole in the leather.

You will also need to have a few hand-stitching needles in different sizes for hand-sewing projects such as hems or edgings. You can usually buy a pack of various sizes at your local sewing shop.

Basic Machine Stitches

You'll use three basic machine stitches when refashioning.

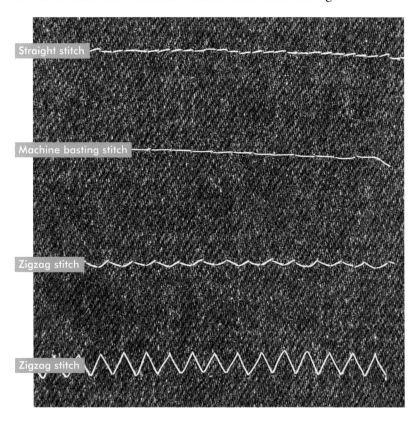

Straight stitch

Machine basting stitch

Zigzag stitch

Zigzag stitch

STRAIGHT STITCH

This stitch is the most basic and the one you'll use the most.

MACHINE BASTING STITCH

This is using the longest stitch length on your machine. This stitch is used to make gathers or to baste something prior to actually sewing it. The large stitches make it easier to remove if need be.

ZIGZAG STITCH

The zigzag stitch moves the needle back and forth when you're stitching. This creates elasticity, so you can use it when you are sewing with knits. You can also use this stitch to neaten a raw edge or even as a decorative stitch. You can adjust your machine to create different widths and lengths of the zigzag stitch.

SEWING A BASIC SEAM

Sewing a seam is one of the most basic of all sewing techniques. A basic straight seam will work well for most purposes. The seam allowance is the distance from the raw edge of the fabric to the line where you are sewing. For example, if a pattern or the directions call for a ⅝″ seam allowance, then you should sew ⅝″ from the raw edge.

1 Pin 2 pieces of fabric together with right sides facing each other and the raw edges aligned.

2 Align the raw edges with the markings on the throat plate of your sewing machine to get the correct seam allowance.

3 Stitch along the desired seam allowance using the throat plate lines as a width guide, backstitching a few stitches at the beginning to secure the seam. Remove the pins as you sew.

4 At the end of your seam, backstitch again to secure the seam. Clip the thread ends.

5 Press the seam allowances open.

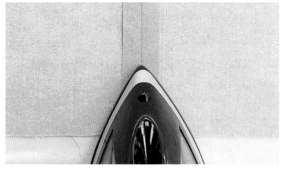

TOPSTITCHING

A nice way to finish off a seam is to machine stitch over each seam allowance, close to the seamline. I used this technique on the Wild Life Jacket (page 64).

1 With the seam allowances pressed open, place the garment in your sewing machine right side up.

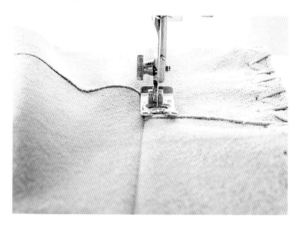

2 Stitch ¼" away from the seamline on each side. Make sure you catch the seam allowance underneath as you sew.

Basic Hand Stitches

SLIP STITCH

A slip stitch is a good way to join layers of fabric or to hem a garment. I used it in Spotlight on the Little Black Dress (page 53).

Using matching thread, bring the thread up through the hem and catch a few threads of the main fabric. Pull the thread tight, go diagonally up through the bottom of the hem, and repeat.

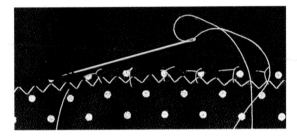

WHIPSTITCH

A whipstitch is used to join two edges together. I used this stitch on the lining of the Renegade Ikat Bag (page 116).

Insert the needle from the back to the front at a diagonal so the thread comes out about ⅛″ away from the previous stitch. Repeat this process along the entire edge.

BLANKET STITCH

The blanket stitch isn't just for blankets, you know. It's also a nice decorative way to finish an edge on anything from felted wool mittens to the Leather Laptop Sleeve (page 112). It's a pretty easy and fast way to spruce up an otherwise boring, plain edge.

1 Thread the needle and knot the end of the thread.

2 Bring the needle up from the wrong side of the material.

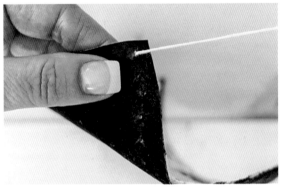

3 Leaving a small loop at the top, take the needle from the wrong side of the material to the right side approximately ¼″ away from your first stitch. Bring the tip of the needle up through the loop at the top edge of the material.

4 Pull the needle until the thread is tight.

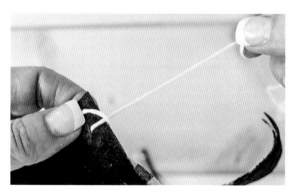

5 Bring the needle back up from the wrong side of the material ¼″ away from the last stitch.

6 Leave a small loop. Bring the needle through the loop.

7 Pull the thread tight again.

8 Keep repeating until you are all the way across, and then knot the end.

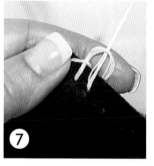
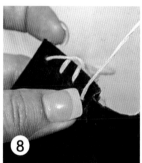

Basic Techniques

Turn Under

You can turn the raw edge under and stitch it down to create a simple hem.

To make a single-fold hem, fold the edge under to the wrong side once and stitch it down. This type of edge finish can be used on fabrics that won't fray.

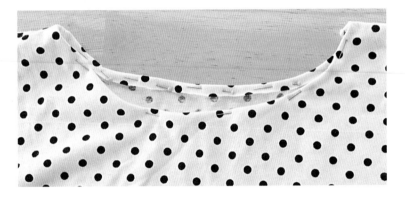

To make a double-fold hem, fold the edge under to the wrong side twice, press, and stitch close to the upper fold. This method hides the raw edge and prevents the fabric from fraying.

Bias Tape

The second way you can finish a raw edge is to attach bias tape. It is a nice way to finish a curved edge.

Bias tape is a strip of fabric cut on the diagonal grain of the fabric. You can make your own bias tape or you can purchase it premade. I used this technique on My New Floral Dress (page 102).

1 Unfold an edge of the bias tape. With raw edges and right sides together, pin the bias tape to the curved edge (in this case, a neckline). Leave ¼″ loose at the beginning to fold under.

2 Sew along the crease in the bias tape that is closest to the raw edge of the neckline.

3 Bring the bias tape up and over the seam allowance to the wrong side. Fold the creased edge under, press, and pin in place.

4 Stitch close to the edge of the bias tape.

HEMMING WITH HEM TAPE

Hem tape, or seam binding, is essentially a lightweight sew-in ribbon or flat lace trim that creates a nice finished edge on your garment. Use it especially when you don't want to add any bulk to your hem. I used hem tape on the Ultra Cashmere Skirt (page 57).

1 Sew close to the new bottom edge of the skirt with a zigzag stitch.

2 Get some coordinating woven-edge seam binding or hem tape that coordinates with your skirt fabric. You can even find sewing notions like this at thrift shops!

3 Place the hem tape on the right side of the bottom edge of the skirt, so that the tape extends ¼" beyond the raw edge of the skirt. Fold the ends of the hem tape underneath themselves and pin in place all around.

4 Stitch the hem tape onto the right side of skirt, close to the upper edge of the tape.

5 Fold the hem ¾″ (or your desired amount) to the wrong side. Press and pin the hem in place.

6 Hem the skirt using a hem stitch. Thread a hand-sewing needle with a single length of matching thread. Bring the needle up through the top of the hem tape at an angle and pick up a few threads of the main fabric.

7 Stitch to the left and diagonally to pick up a few threads of the hem.

8 Continue stitching this way around the entire hem.

MAKING A FRENCH SEAM

A French seam is an enclosed seam—it is a nice seam finish for sheer fabrics or materials prone to fraying, and it works best for straight seams. I used it on the Headlight Halter Dress (page 48).

1 Pin fabric pieces *wrong* sides together.

2 Stitch together with a ¼″ seam allowance.

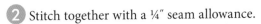

3 Press the seam allowances open.

4 Flip the sewn pieces so the *right* sides are together now, and press the seam again with an iron.

5 With right sides together, sew a ½″ seam. This makes a seam allowance of ¾″ per side (1½″ total). You can also make a French seam with both seam allowances only ¼″, or with a ¼″ seam allowance first, then a ⅜″ seam allowance (which corresponds to the typical ⅝″ allowed for in garment patterns).

6 Open and press seam to the side (usually whichever direction will be down or toward the back when the garment is worn).

7 With these wider French seams, I take the extra step of edge-stitching along the free side of my French seam to make sure it stays smooth (see Topstitching, page 25).

INSTALLING A CENTERED ZIPPER

1 With a regular stitch, sew the seam up to where the zipper will end.

2 Switch your machine to the longest stitch length, and machine baste along the seamline where the zipper will be installed.

TIP

You can shorten a zipper from the bottom. Mark the new end point, stitch across the zipper teeth several times by hand with sturdy thread to make a new stop, and cut the zipper off a little below your stitching. Then follow the steps in Installing a Centered Zipper (at left) to install your zipper.

3 Press the seam open.

4 Open the zipper and place it face down on the wrong side of the seam, directly over the basting stitches. Line up the teeth of the zipper with the seamline.

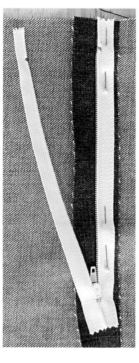

6 Stop when you get to the bottom of the zipper.

7 Zip the zipper pull up to the top of the zipper.

5 Use a zipper foot and, starting at the top, stitch down a side of the zipper.

8 Pivot and sew a small line of stitches across the bottom of the zipper.

9 Pivot again and continue stitching back up to the top of the zipper.

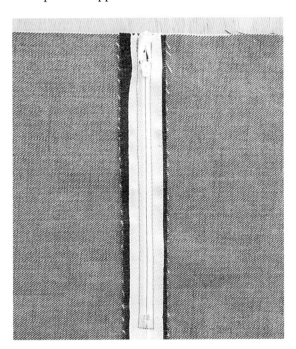

10 Use a seam ripper to remove the basting stitches.

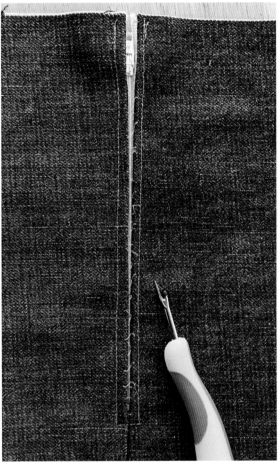

ADDING DARTS

Darts will create curves in your garment. When sewing with a commercial pattern, you will be given the precise place to put a dart. When you are refashioning, you'll need to place darts where you think they need to go. I usually use them in the top of my skirts to bring in the waistline a bit and allow room for my backside. But you can also use them to bring in the waistline of a shirt.

This demonstration is for a set of ½″ darts. Your darts may need to be smaller or larger, depending on how much fullness you need.

1 Using chalk, mark 3″ and 3½″ from the center back of the skirt waist. Mark these distances on both sides of the center line.

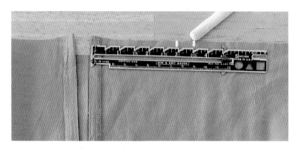

2 Repeat Step 1 on the center front of the skirt waist.

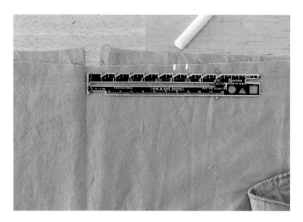

3 Measure 4″ down from the center of the 2 marks you made, and make a mark with chalk. Do this for all 4 darts.

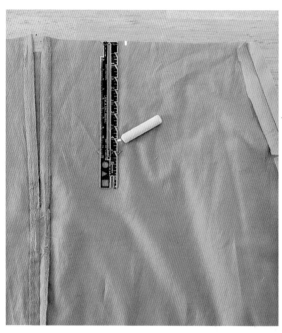

4 Fold fabric in half with right sides together. Match the two upper marks. Pin at the bottom 4″ mark and at the top.

5 Do this for all 4 darts.

6 Starting at the top of the dart, stitch at an angle all the way down to your 4″ mark. Do not backstitch. If you hand tie this knot, the dart will lie flat.

7 Hand tie the bottom knot.

8 Press the darts toward the center.

GATHERING

Gathering is a good way to bring in a waistline of a skirt when you aren't using darts. It creates a more full look and is nice when you are using elastic like I did on the Great Art Skirt (page 72).

1 Using the longest stitch on your machine, baste across the edge of the piece you want to gather. Leave long thread tails and do *not* backstitch at either end of your stitching.

2 Gently pull the bobbin (bottom) thread to gather the fabric until it is the desired size. Adjust the gathers so they are even. Knot the ends of the gathering threads or wrap them around a pin placed in the fabric to keep the gathers in place.

Now you are ready to attach a waistband of your choice.

MAKING CAP SLEEVES

One nice and easy way to finish off a refashioned garment is to add cap sleeves. I used this sleeve on the Date Night Dress (page 42) and the Emerald Petals Dress (page 108).

1 Cut 2 rectangles of coordinating fabric 5″ × 12″.

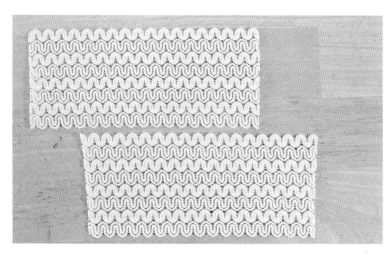

2 Fold each rectangle in half.

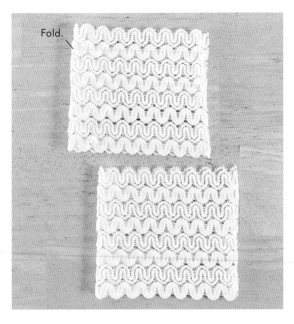

3 Starting at the fold, cut in an arc down to the opposite corner.

4 Hem the long side of the fabric if needed. Mark the top point of the arc with a washable marking pen.

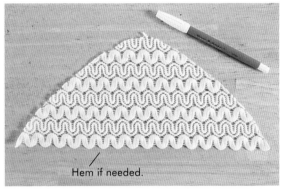

5 Matching the top mark with the shoulder seam, pin the rounded edge of the sleeve under the existing armhole edge.

6 Stitch along the pin line.

Projects

Date Night Dress

What You Will Do

Combine part of a dress (skirt) and a coordinating fabric (bodice) to make a dress

Refashion Techniques

→ Make a dress using a pattern

→ Remove and reinstall a zipper

→ Add darts to a skirt

→ Attach a bodice to a skirt

→ Add cap sleeves

Shhhhhhhhhhh! Do you hear that? Please tell me I'm not the only one who hears the clothes at thrift shops and garage sales! I hear their chatter constantly. Some of the quality designer garments are proud of where they came from but shocked to now be scattered among the poorly made, worn-out clothes. "How did I get here?" they ask me. Or sometimes, the bad ones will plead with me, like this green muumuu. It hollered my name from all the way across the old plastic food storage containers at the garage sale. "Beth, take me home! You know you love my color! You know there's hope for me! Please don't leave me here destined for the rag bag or, even worse, the dump!" I just couldn't leave it there. I had to take it home with me. My husband thinks I'm crazy, but I really do hear their voices.

Once in a while an old pattern will beg me to take it home, too. And no, I'm not getting married, but just look at the nice bodice on the pattern I

used. I'm pretty sure I can combine this with the green muumuu for a perfect date night dress.

My friend Linda, who also hears the voices, gifted me with this cool thrift store lace that she found years ago. I knew if I combined it with the white thrifted lining material it would make the perfect bodice for the dress I had in mind.

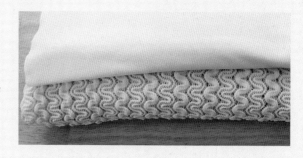

① Once you've found the perfect too-large dress to refashion, use a seam ripper to take out the zipper. Set the zipper aside for later.

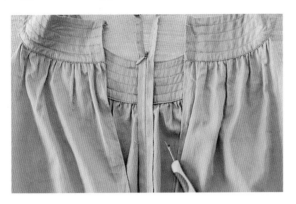

You can use any pencil or straight skirt pattern for the bottom of this dress. I highly recommend spending the time to learn how to draft a custom pencil skirt pattern for yourself. I use mine all the time, combining it with different bodices and fabrics to create many new looks.

② Fold the front of the muumuu in half. Lay the front pattern piece on the CF (center front) fold, matching up the bottom of the pattern and the bottom of the dress. Pin and cut out the front panel of the skirt.

This what the front piece will look like. I think it's feeling better already, don't you?

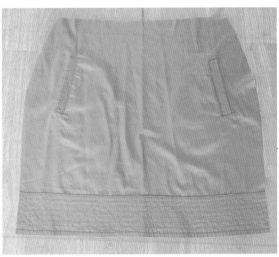

③ Fold the back of the muumuu in half so the back seam is on the CB (center back) fold. Lay the back pattern piece on the fold, aligning it at the bottom, and pin and cut out the back panel of the skirt.

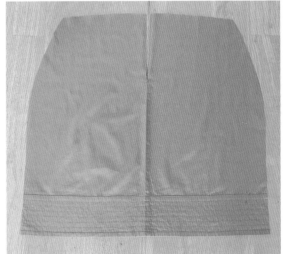

4 With right sides together, pin the skirt front to the skirt back at the sides.

5 Starting at the bottom, sew the sides together with a ½" seam. This will keep the hem of the skirt even.

6 Make 2 darts, each ½", in the front of the skirt, 3" from either side of the CF (see Adding Darts, page 37).

7 Make 2 darts, each ½", in the back of the skirt, 3" from either side of the CB.

8 Construct the bodice using the directions from the pattern of your choice. When I am using a new pattern, I always make a muslin (a trial garment, often made of inexpensive muslin fabric) from an old sheet first to see if I need to make any adjustments to the pattern before I actually use my fabric. Make sure the bodice and your new skirt will fit together smoothly. The bodice of this pattern just happened to fit perfectly with no adjustments needed. YAY!

9 Fold the bottom edge of the bodice and the lining both ½" to the wrong side. Press lightly. Tuck the upper, raw edge of the skirt inside the folded edges of the lining and the main fabric of the bodice. Pin all 3 layers together.

10 Sew all 3 layers together, topstitching close to the folded edge of the bodice.

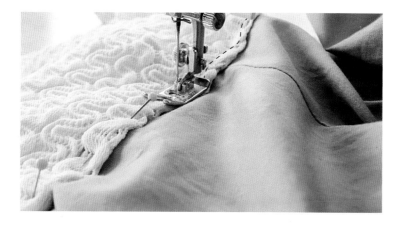

11 Install the zipper (see Installing a Centered Zipper, page 34).

12 Add sleeves if you desire (see Making Cap Sleeves, page 39).

Now, after I get home from a nice dinner out with my husband, the dress just smiles and says things to me like, "Hey, that restaurant was great. I can't wait to see where we are going next!" Such a rewarding hobby, don't you think?

Headlight Halter Dress

What You Will Do

Shorten a dress and redesign the bodice

Refashion Techniques

→ Shorten a dress

→ Redesign a bodice using a pattern

→ Install a zipper

→ Attach a bodice to a skirt

I know exactly what you're thinking. Is this the before or the after? It's such a cute maxi dress, why would she want to refashion it? Why would someone donate that beautiful dress to the thrift shop? I know, I asked myself those same questions. Until I noticed the headlights. Yep, headlights. Look closely at the pattern on the bust. Yikes! Someone didn't think about the pattern placement very well.

OK, now, that being said, I still liked it and thought I could ignore the glaring headlights,

hope no one else would notice them, and wear it as a maxi dress anyway. My plan was to wear it around the house and see if I was comfortable in it. Well, every time I sat down, the elastic back of the dress would pull down to expose yet another unmentionable part of my body. Plan B was to make it into a maxi skirt. But I really wanted those beautiful colors up around my face. By the end of the day, I had made my decision. This little beauty was going to become a knee-length halter dress. There were plenty of other maxis in the sea.

1 Measure the distance from your waist (or wherever you want the seam between bodice and skirt to fall—mine is an empire waist) to your desired hemline (see Measuring for Fit, page 20). Add ½″ to this measurement for the seam allowance. Use a measuring tape to mark this distance with chalk, from the bottom of the hem up, all around the dress. Cut off the bottom of the dress, using the chalk line as a guide. This will become your new skirt. Set it aside for later.

Sometimes when refashioning, you can use a commercial pattern for part of the garment. In this case, I planned to use part of a halter pattern I had in my collection for the halter top of the dress.

2 Cut off the rest of the fabric right under the existing bodice. This will give you a nice piece of fabric to use for your halter pattern pieces.

When working with commercial patterns, I always make a muslin first. This way I can make any adjustments before I cut out my fabric. After tweaking the pattern ever so slightly, I had my pattern pieces and I was ready to cut. This is when I check and double-check just to make sure everything is right, since there is no room for error.

3 Pin the pattern pieces in place on the fabric you cut off in Step 2 according to the pattern directions. Cut them out. Cut out any lining pieces from remaining scraps or a coordinating fabric, if needed.

4 Follow the sewing instructions for the halter pattern you used to make the new bodice.

5 On the upper raw edge of the cut-off skirt, baste all around the edge, leaving long thread tails. This will create gathers so you can ease your skirt to fit the halter bodice (see Gathering, page 39).

6 With right sides together, pin the top of the skirt to the bodice. Be sure to match the side seams and the center front and back. Pull on the bobbin thread of the basting stitch to gather the top of the skirt to fit the bodice.

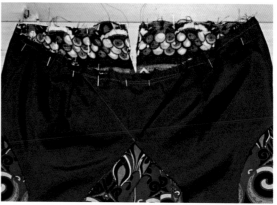

7 Sew the bodice and skirt together with a ½" seam allowance.

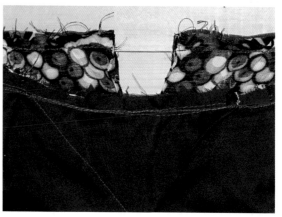

8 Attach seam binding on the raw edge of this seam (see Bias Tape, page 29).

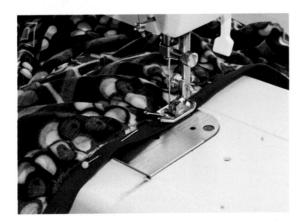

9 Find a zipper to match your dress that is 16″ long. Using a seam ripper, open up the center back seam from the top down to fit the zipper.

10 Install the zipper (see Installing a Centered Zipper, page 34).

I feel much more comfortable in my new dress. I'm pretty sure people will now be looking at my face and the cute new halter dress instead of being distracted.

Spotlight on the Little Black Dress

What You Will Do

Shorten a dress and redesign the bodice

Refashion Techniques

→ Remove a collar

→ Shorten a dress

I love a good polka dot, and the nautical look really rolls my socks up and down, but this dress was just too much of a good thing. I probably would have worn this dress when I started teaching in 1990. However, I could hear a still, quiet voice rising up from under all that 90s goodness. It was politely asking me to bring it out of a world of obscurity and into the classy world of the modern LBD. Naturally, I had to say yes and give it a try.

Surprise! The collar was actually a tie-on vest, just attached at the shoulders. This will be an easy fix.

1 Use your trusty seam ripper to remove the vest from the shoulder seams. A conventional collar can be removed in a similar way.

2 Remove any shoulder pads with your seam ripper.

3 Pin the shoulder seams back together and sew along the original seamline. If you removed a conventional collar, pin the neckline seams back together and sew along the original seamline.

4 Measure from the waistline to your desired hem length (see Measuring for Fit, page 20), add 1″ for a hem allowance, and mark this length all around the dress with chalk.

5 Use the chalk line as a guide and cut off the bottom of the dress.

6 Use a zigzag stitch to sew all around the new bottom raw edge of the dress.

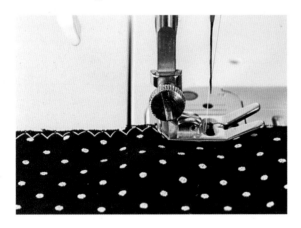

7 Fold the hem under 1″ toward the wrong side, pin if needed, and press.

8 Using matching thread, slipstitch the hem in place (see Slip Stitch, page 26).

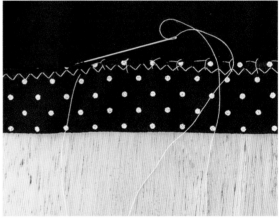

I can hear a big sigh of relief and gratitude coming from this now-classy, professional, and modern little black dress that can be worn to work or for an evening out. I don't think I'll ever get tired of seeing the difference a few simple changes will make for an outfit.

Ultra Cashmere Skirt

What You Will Do

Shorten a skirt

Refashion Techniques

→ Cut off and rehem a skirt

At first, I didn't even notice the skirt as I walked past it at the thrift store. I was heading straight for a navy blue polka dot shirt. I stopped in my tracks when I felt it reach out and softly brush my arm and quietly whisper my name. "Beth, feel how soft I am. Wouldn't you like to take me home with you? Look at my wonderful pleats and my muted stripes." I was immediately mesmerized by this smooth-talking skirt. At once, I could see beyond the wrinkled frumpiness of it all. I couldn't help but caress it as I headed for the checkout stand.

The labels look a little 70s to me. I wish I knew more about this brand, but my Google search didn't give me much information.

I think a little shortening and a bit of pressing is all I need to do to make this skirt more modern.

1 Mark the desired new length plus ½″ for a hem with chalk all around the skirt, on each pleat. It's much easier to mark a skirt that isn't pleated!

2 Use your chalk marks as a guide to cut off the bottom of the skirt.

3 Hem the skirt with hem tape (see Hemming with Hem Tape, page 30).

4 Press the pleats back in with a hot steam iron.

Just try to keep yourself from reaching out and stroking me as I walk past you in this skirt combined with the Merino Wool Cardigan (page 60). I dare you!

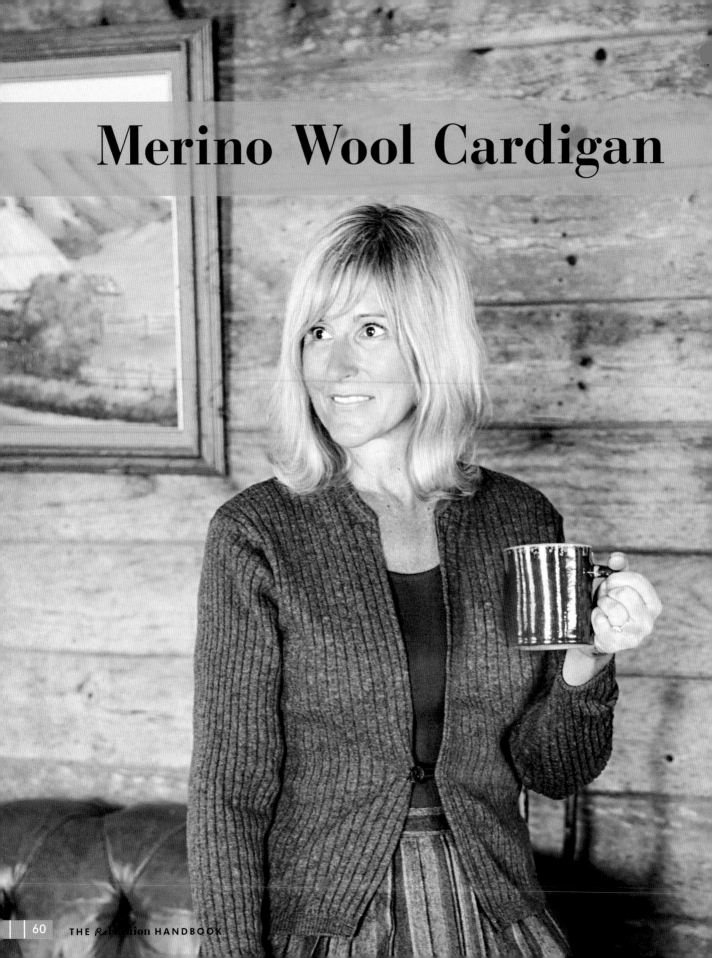

Merino Wool Cardigan

What You Will Do

Make a pullover sweater into a cardigan

Refashion Techniques

→ Create a front opening

→ Finish the edges of a new front opening

→ Add a button closure

I usually can't wear wool right against my skin. But this soft Merino wool thrift store sweater is a whole different story. I wish you could feel the softness. I loved how it felt, but pullover sweaters don't do much for me. It was destined to become more flattering as a cardigan.

1 Using scissors, cut up the center front of the sweater.

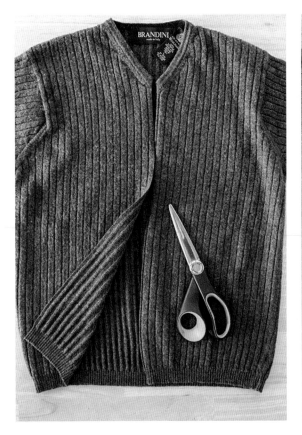

3 With right sides together, pin the lace to the raw edges of the sweater's new opening.

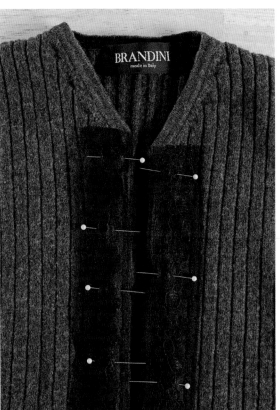

2 Cut 2 pieces of lace the same length as the front opening of the sweater. If you're worried the lace will fray, seal the ends with Fray Check and let it dry before doing anything else.

④ Select a button and a hair elastic that match your sweater. Cut the hair elastic in half.

⑤ Decide where you would like the sweater to fasten. Mark the placement for the button ¾" in from one edge. Fold the hair elastic in half. At the same place on the opposite side of the sweater opening, tuck the cut ends under the lace strip and pin in place.

⑥ Sew the lace strips to the sweater along the cut edges with a ¼" seam allowance.

⑦ Fold the lace over along the seamline to the wrong side of the sweater.

⑧ Pin the lace to the wrong side of the opening. Topstitch around all 4 sides of the lace about ¼" from the edge.

⑨ Sew on the button.

Now I'll stay nice and toasty this winter, and the sweater goes perfectly with the Ultra Cashmere Skirt (page 57).

Wild Life Jacket

What You Will Do

Take in and shorten a leather jacket

Refashion Techniques

→ Disassemble, take in, and reassemble a jacket

→ Shorten a jacket by adding a waist seam

Instead of the voices, this time I heard the sounds of wildlife when I walked past this huge but soft and velvety leather jacket. I heard elk bugling, coyotes howling, and birds chirping. I looked around expecting to see Dr. Dolittle following behind me, but instead the jacket smiled, waved, and gave me its cute look. How could I not take it home and remake it into something fun? It had wonderful details, but it was too big.

1 Determine how much shorter you want the new jacket to be, and write this number down.

2 Determine and mark the new waistline. Allowing for a ½″ seam allowance below the waistline mark, cut off the jacket at the new waistline. You'll need the cut-off section later, so keep it handy.

3 Measure from your wrist to your shoulder to determine the new sleeve length. Cut the sleeves off the jacket at the shoulder, keeping track of which sleeve is which. Remove the lining, and mark the new sleeve length from the hem up.

4 Turn the jacket inside out and place on your dress form. Remove any lining and shoulder pads.

5 Pin the side seams and shoulder seams to fit. Try the jacket on inside out to check the fit and adjust as needed.

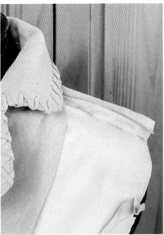

6 Using a leather needle in your sewing machine, sew a straight seam along each pin line on the side seams and shoulder seams. Trim along the new seams, leaving a ½″ seam allowance.

7 Using the marks from Step 3, cut off the top of each sleeve.

8 With right sides together, pin each sleeve back into the corresponding armhole. Match the underarm seams with the side seams, and the centers of the sleeve tops with the shoulder seams. Sew together all around the armhole.

9 From the top of the cut-off section of jacket, cut away the amount by which you want to shorten the jacket (from Step 1).

10 With right sides and raw edges together, pin and sew the shortened jacket bottom to the new jacket waist. If the bottom strip is too large, you can make it fit the waist it by sewing a seam or a dart (see Adding Darts, page 37) in the back before you reattach it to the jacket.

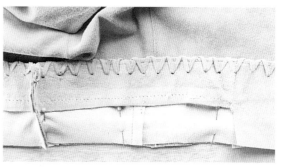

11 Topstitch above and below the new waist seam (see Topstitching, page 25).

12 *Optional:* Finish the new seams with bias tape (see Bias Tape, page 29).

Pair this with the Wild Life Skirt (page 68) and some leather wedges for a fun, wild look.

Wild Life Skirt

What You Will Do

Take in and shorten an elastic-waist skirt

Refashion Techniques

→ Remove and replace a sewn-in elastic waistband

→ Take in a skirt

→ Shorten a skirt without changing the original hem

Sometimes a few simple resizing alterations are all it takes to make thrift store clothes work—like this wonderful wild print skirt. It reminded me of a jungle print. I loved the idea of leather with the jungle print, so I decided to resize this to wear with the leather Wild Life Jacket (page 64).

1 Cut the entire waistband off the skirt, just below the elastic.

2 Cut the elastic waistband to your waist size plus ½″.

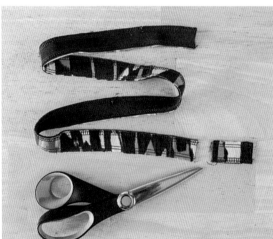

3 Overlap the ends of the elastic by ½", and stitch together using a zigzag stitch.

4 From the bottom of the skirt up, mark your desired skirt length around the skirt using a washable marking pen. Use the line as a guide and cut the skirt away above the marks.

5 Measure around the new top of the skirt. Subtract your waist size from the circumference of the skirt. Write this number down—this will be how much width you need to remove.

6 If your skirt has 2 side seams:

> Divide the number from Step 5 by 4 (the number of seam allowances) to give you the distance you'll need to come in on both sides.
>
> For example:
>
> New top of skirt = 39″
>
> Your waist size = 31″
>
> 39″ – 31″ = 8″; 8″ ÷ 4 = 2″
>
> You'll need to sew new seams 2″ in from the existing side seams.

If your skirt has only a center back seam:

> Divide the number from Step 5 by 2 (the number of seam allowances) to give you the distance you'll need to come in at the back.
>
> For example:
>
> New top of skirt = 39″
>
> Your waist size = 31″
>
> 39″ – 31″ = 8″; 8″ ÷ 2 = 4″
>
> You'll need to sew a new seam 4″ in from the existing center back seam.

7 Sew the new seams based on the number you determined in Step 6.

8 Trim off the extra fabric from the seams, leaving a ½" seam allowance.

9 Pin the elastic waistband onto the top of the skirt, both wrong sides together.

10 Using a zigzag stitch, sew the elastic waistband to the skirt.

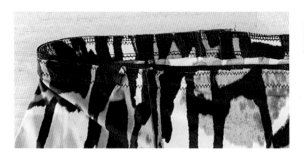

11 Fold the waistband over to the wrong side of the skirt. Using a needle and thread, hand tack the elastic down at each seam.

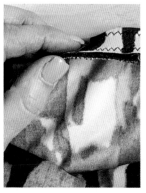 

Much better fit now.

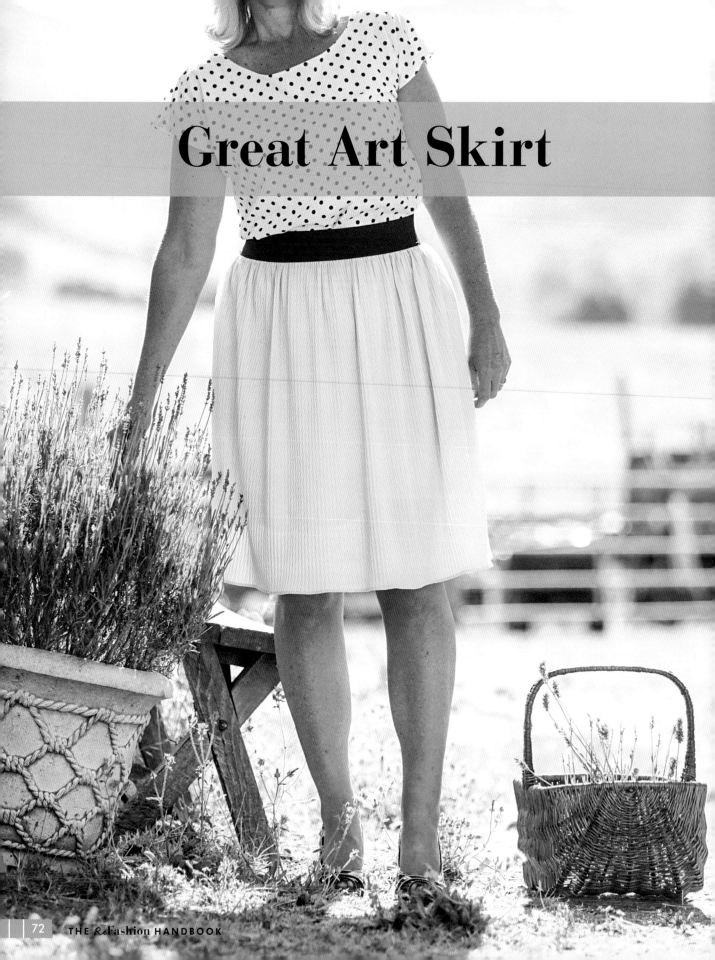

Great Art Skirt

What You Will Do

Make a skirt from a dress

Refashion Techniques

→ Cut off the bottom of a dress to make a skirt

→ Remove extra width to narrow a skirt

→ Add a sewn-in elastic waistband

For some reason, when I first put on this dress, I had a strong desire to grab a hymnal, run up on some risers, and start belting out my rendition of "How Great Thou Art." Seeing as my voice is not something that would lift your spirit toward the heavens, I decided to spare you and stick to what I'm good at—sewing. And look at those delicious small pleats—this just had to be saved.

The bottom of the dress will become the new skirt, so you could even follow these techniques for a dress that is too small on top, as long as the fullness of the skirt will fit over your hips.

1 Measure the distance from your waist to your desired hemline (see Measuring for Fit, page 20) and add ½″ for a seam allowance. Use your measuring tape to mark this distance, from the hem of the dress up, with a washable marking pen.

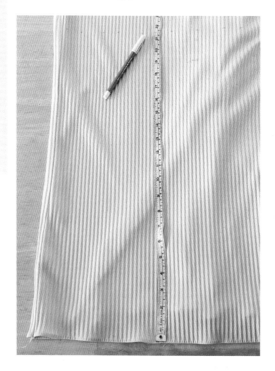

2 Cut all across the bottom of the dress using your marks as a guide. The section you cut off will be your new skirt.

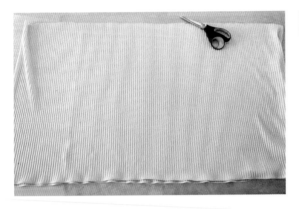

3 To determine the new fullness of the skirt, measure the largest part of your hips and add anywhere from a quarter to half of that measurement, depending on how full you'd like the skirt, plus an extra 1″ for the seam allowance. Cut along a seam of the skirt to yield a flat piece of fabric instead of a tube. Then cut off the excess from the side of the skirt to yield a piece the measurement you determined.

4 Use the longest stitch on your machine to sew a basting stitch all across the top of the skirt piece, but don't gather it yet.

5 With right sides together, resew the side of the skirt with a ½″ seam allowance.

6 Cut a piece of 2″-wide knit elastic your waist size plus ½″. Overlap the ends ½″ and use a zigzag stitch to connect the ends of the elastic.

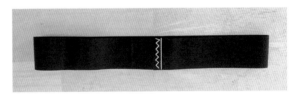

7 Mark the elastic waistband in quarters (center front, center back, and 2 sides). Mark the top of the skirt in quarters as well.

8 Matching the marks, pin the top of the right side of the skirt to the bottom of the wrong side of the elastic waistband. Make sure the overlap on the elastic waistband is at the center back of the skirt. Pull the bobbin thread of your basting stitch and gather the skirt to fit the waistband.

9 Attach the elastic to the skirt using a zigzag stitch.

Now, I think this outfit will be easier on your eyes and ears because when I put this on I feel like heading over to the Nightingale Gallery to view some great art instead of singing "How Great Thou Art" tonight.

QUICK AND EASY
T-Shirt Resize

What You Will Do

Reshape a T-shirt

Refashion Techniques

→ Take in the sides of a T-shirt

→ Remove and finish a neckline and sleeve edges

There are barrels of oversized, shapeless T-shirts at thrift stores, like this unflattering, huge T-shirt, whose only redeeming feature is the polka dots. T-shirts make great beginner projects because you can buy them for next to nothing, there are thousands of patterns and designs, and they don't fray when you cut them, which makes seam finishing a snap.

1 Cut off both sleeves at the seams. Cut off the neck band.

2 Turn the T-shirt inside out and pin the sides to fit the way you like. If you don't have a dress form, you can put it on yourself and have a friend pin it for you.

4 Try on the shirt to make sure it fits, then trim the seams to a ½″ seam allowance.

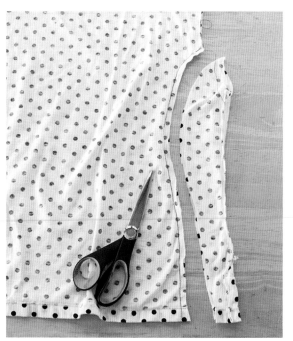

5 Turn the neckline and armhole openings over ¼″ to the wrong side, pin, and sew down close to the raw edge using a straight stitch.

3 With right sides together, use the pin lines as a guide to sew the new side seams. Remove the pins as you sew.

Now you have a fun, flattering, versatile new T-shirt that you can wear with jeans or dress up and wear with a skirt.

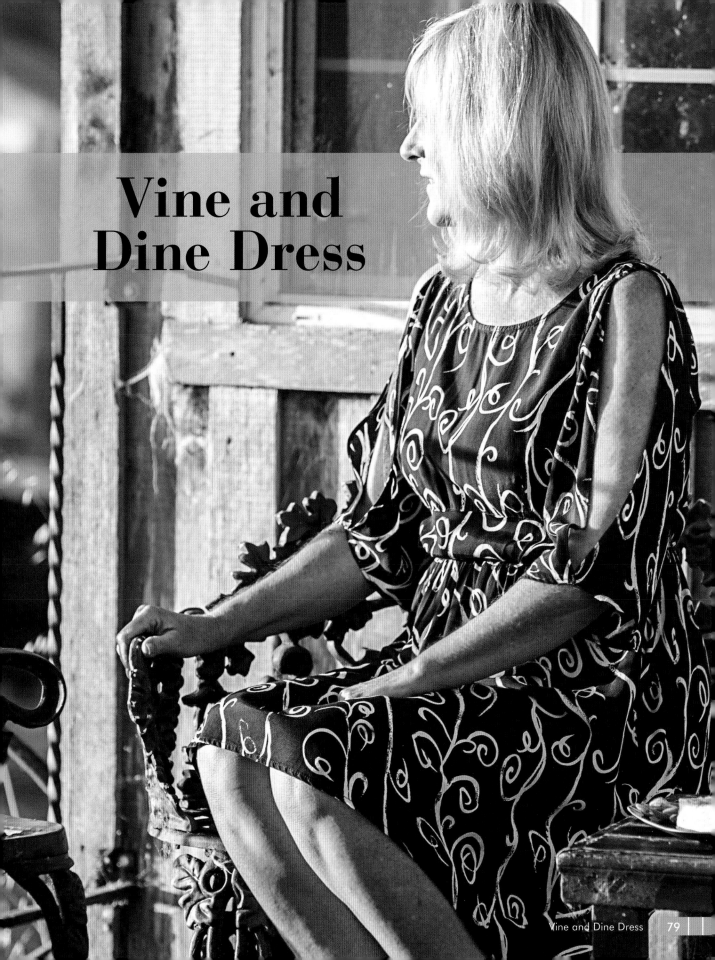

Vine and Dine Dress

Refashion Techniques

→ Shorten a dress by removing its middle section

→ Gather and add elastic at a waistline

→ Reattach a bodice and skirt

→ Make sleeves from cut-off fabric and add them to a dress

Here's another thrift store dress that just didn't do much for my figure. If I remember correctly, the vine-looking swirl pattern and the fact that it was black and white were the only things that drew me to it in the first place. Other than that, there was not much personality there.

1 Measure from your shoulder to your waistline (see Measuring for Fit, page 20) and add ½″ for a seam allowance. Measure this distance on your dress and mark all across with a piece of chalk. Cut on this line.

2 Measure yourself to determine your desired new skirt length (see Measuring for Fit, page 20), and add ½″ for a seam allowance. Mark this distance, from the hem up, all around the skirt. Cut on this line.

This will become the new skirt of the dress. You basically just cut out the middle of the dress.

3 Use the longest stitch on your machine to baste all around the top of the skirt.

4 Pull the bobbin thread to gather the skirt to fit the bottom of the bodice. With the right sides together, pin the bottom of the bodice to the top of the skirt, easing the skirt to fit.

5 Sew the bodice and skirt, right sides together, with a ½″ seam allowance.

6 Cut a piece of ¼″-wide elastic the same length as your waist minus 3″. Mark the elastic in quarters. Pin the center mark to the center front of the *waist seam allowance*, the quarter marks to the side seams, and the ends to the center back. Using a zigzag stitch on your machine, start sewing the elastic at the center back to the *seam allowance only*, stretching the elastic as you sew to match each of the marks.

7 If your dress has sleeves, cut them off neatly just past the armscye (armhole opening) seam and set them aside. Measure the circumference of the armscye and make sure the piece you cut from the middle of the dress is at least equal to that measurement. Decide on a new sleeve length and make sure it will fit, too.

8 Using the extra piece you cut from the middle of the dress, cut one side off at a 90° angle as shown. Using the measurements from Step 7, measure over and down the length from Step 7 and cut off the other side (and bottom, if needed) to make 2 rectangles. These will become the new sleeves.

⑨ To finish the sleeve slits, fold and press each long edge over ¼″ to the wrong side twice, to hide the raw edges.

⑩ Sew along each long edge to hem the sleeve slits.

⑪ If your fabric has a directional pattern, determine what end of each rectangle should be the bottom of the sleeve. Repeat Steps 9 and 10 to hem the bottom of each sleeve rectangle.

⑫ With a hand-sewing needle and matching thread, tack the 2 bottom corners together on each sleeve.

⑬ Fold each sleeve in half lengthwise and mark the center of the upper edge with a pin. Place a sleeve under an existing armhole seam, aligning the pin with the side seam of the bodice. Pin in place, leaving the sleeve slit open at the top. Topstitch around the armhole seam to attach the sleeve.

The new sleeves and shorter length make this dress much more interesting and perfect for dinner or a night out.

TRIBAL TIE-DYE
Maxi Dress

What You Will Do

Make a skirt and add it to a refashioned shirt to make a dress

Refashion Techniques

→ Make a skirt from yardage

→ Shorten a shirt to make a dress bodice

→ Attach a bodice to a skirt

→ Add a sewn-in elastic waistband

Two of the most popular posts on my blog, The Renegade Seamstress, are the maxi dress posts. It seems appropriate to include at least one maxi dress for you in this book. This is a more dressy version of the "Easy DIY Maxi Dress in Fifteen Minutes or Less" from The Renegade Seamstress.

While shopping one day, I was completely mesmerized by this lightweight, tribal-print knit fabric. Immediately, my mind went to a too-short lightweight knit shirt that had been sitting in my closet for years. I loved the neckline of the shirt and wanted to let it see the light of day again by combining it with this fabric to make a maxi dress. When refashioning, don't forget to "shop" your closet for unworn or ill-fitting clothes that you might use in your creation. You can make brand new outfits when you combine your old clothes with some fun fabric.

1 Mark where the shirt hits your waistline. Add ½″ for a seam allowance. Cut the excess length away from the bottom of the shirt.

2 Measure from your waistline to the floor (see Measuring for Fit, page 20) and add 1½″ for seam allowances and a hem. This will be the length to cut your skirt fabric.

3 Measure around your waistline and multiply by 1.5. This will be the width to cut your fabric.

4 Cut a rectangle from the skirt fabric to these measurements.

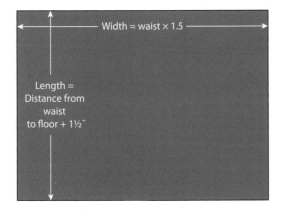

Width = waist × 1.5

Length = Distance from waist to floor + 1½″

5 Fold the skirt rectangle in half through the length, right sides together. Sew a ½″ seam down the length of the rectangle. The seam will be the center back of the skirt.

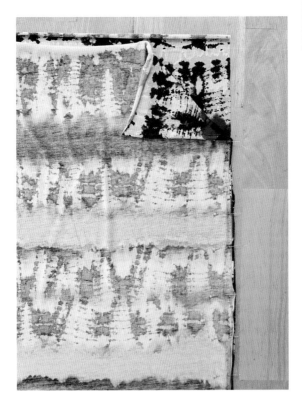

6 Use the longest stitch on your machine to baste around the top of the skirt.

7 Mark the bottom of the shirt in quarters (center front, center back, and 2 sides). Mark the top of the skirt in quarters as well. Tuck the shirt inside the top of the skirt, with raw edges and right sides together, matching and pinning at the marks. Pull the bobbin thread of your basting stitch and gather until the top of the skirt fits the shirt. Pin all around.

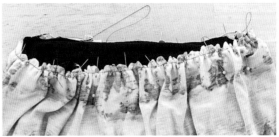

8 Using a zigzag stitch, sew the skirt to the shirt with a ½″ seam allowance.

9 Measure and cut a piece of ¼″-wide elastic equal to the shirt's waistline circumference minus 3″. Using a washable marker or pins, mark the elastic in half and then in quarters.

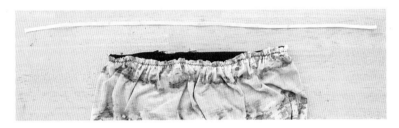

10 Using the quarter marks on the skirt from Step 7, pin the elastic to the seam allowance at the marks with the cut ends at the center back.

11 Using a zigzag stitch and stretching slightly so the marks will match while you sew, sew the elastic onto the waistline seam allowance.

12 Hem the skirt with a ½″ double-fold hem.

I love the tribal tie-dye look of this maxi dress. I could dress this up or wear it with a cropped jeans jacket for a more casual look.

Detailed Denim Jacket

Refashion Techniques

→ Cut out the back of a jacket

→ Position and attach a decorative piece

→ Sew heavyweight fabrics

So often, I'd love to know the story behind the items I find at thrift stores. I wish garments would tell me their history, in addition to asking me to bring them into this century—like this huge unfinished crewel embroidery piece I found for 50 cents at my local thrift store. I wonder who spent so much time lovingly embroidering this. And what were the maker's plans for it? Who knows, but at least I can feel good about resurrecting it from a dark grocery-bag existence and bringing it out to see the light of day.

Crewel embroidery is stitched with wool threads. Someone worked so hard on this. It wasn't something I knew how to finish, nor was it something I would hang up in my house. I did, however, want to somehow showcase the beautiful handiwork, so putting it in the back of my plain thrift store jeans jacket seemed like a fun solution.

1 Trace the back panel of the jacket, just inside the seams, onto a piece of paper. Cut it out on the lines to make your pattern.

2 Place the pattern over the area of the embroidered piece you'd like to use. Use a wash-away fabric marker to trace around the pattern.

3 Stitch directly on top of your marker lines. This will keep the embroidery from unraveling after you've trimmed the piece down later.

4 Cut out the back panel of the jacket, cutting as close to the seamline as possible. You can use Fray Check on the cut edges to keep it from fraying.

5 Place the jacket on top of the embroidered panel, both right side up. Line up your marked and stitched lines with the seams of the jacket.

6 Pin the embroidered piece in place as shown.

7 Using a heavy-duty 110/18 needle, stitch through the seam, attaching the crewel embroidery piece to the jacket.

8 Trim away the excess embroidered fabric, leaving a ½" seam allowance.

9 Use Fray Check again around the raw edges of the embroidered piece to keep it from fraying.

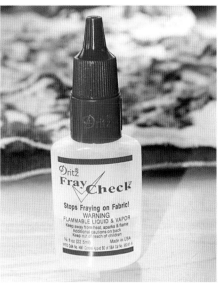

Now, wouldn't it be fun to be out and about, and have the person who originally stitched the embroidery notice it and come tell me the story? I really hope that happens!

Mocha Flow Dress

What You Will Do

Combine a shirt and skirt to make a dress

Refashion Techniques

→ Shorten a skirt

→ Redesign a shirt to make a bodice

→ Alter a skirt lining

→ Attach a bodice to a skirt

→ Attach a sewn-in elastic waistband

This original skirt did not have the most flattering silhouette. The bias cut just seemed to make it cling to all the parts of me I'd rather hide. But somehow, I just can't resist a good polka dot. Then add the fact that it is a mocha brown and cream, and you just can't go wrong, in my opinion. Just like Marc Jacobs said, "There is never a wrong time for a polka dot." Oh, how right you are, Marc! I combined the polka dot skirt with this cream-colored thrift store knit shirt with a nice neckline that was in my stash. To me, it was the perfect mix.

1 Measure from your waistline to your desired hem length (see Measuring for Fit, page 20). Add ½″ for a seam allowance and mark this distance, from the bottom of the skirt up, all across the skirt. Cut on the line. If your skirt is lined, cut the lining at the same time as the outer skirt and keep them together.

2 Measure from your shoulder to your waistline (see Measuring for Fit, page 20). Add ½″ for a seam allowance, mark this distance all across the bottom of the shirt, and cut on the line.

3 Pin the top of the skirt and lining together.

4 Use the longest stitch on your machine to baste across the top of the skirt and the lining.

5 Fold the shirt in half, lining up the side seams, and mark the center front and center back at the bottom. Repeat with the skirt.

6 Tuck the shirt down inside the skirt, with right sides together. Line up the raw edges, matching the side seams, the center fronts, and the center backs. Adjust the skirt to fit the top by pulling the bobbin thread of the basting stitches as needed to gather it. Pin in place all around.

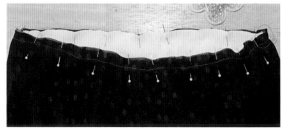

7 Stitch all 3 layers together using a zigzag stitch and a ½″ seam allowance.

8 Cut a piece of ¼″-wide elastic to your waist size minus 3″.

9 Use a washable marking pen to mark the elastic in half and then in quarters.

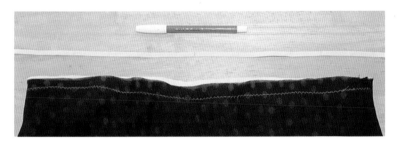

10 With the cut ends at the center back, and matching the quarter marks to the center front and side seams, pin the elastic to the waistline seam allowance.

11 Using a zigzag stitch and keeping the marks lined up, stretch the elastic slightly as you sew it to the waistline so the waistline of the dress stays flat.

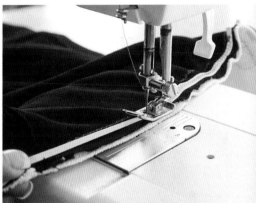

I love how the skirt flows and now flatters my bottom half. This is a much better silhouette for my body type. I pair it with some vintage riding shoes, and I can wear this dress anywhere.

Bow-Sleeve Shirt

What You Will Do

Refashion a T-shirt

Refashion Techniques

→ Take in a T-shirt

→ Make a new neckline

→ Remove, redesign, and reattach sleeves

There are plenty of boxy T-shirts out there just waiting for you to spruce them up a bit. The only redeeming feature of this T-shirt was the color of the stripes. It just wasn't doing it for me, so it was the perfect candidate for refashioning.

1 Cut off the sleeves at the seams and put them aside for later. Put the T-shirt on your dress form inside out or put it on yourself and have a friend help you. Pin the sides to fit.

2 Stitch along your side pin lines, removing the pins as you sew.

3 Put the T-shirt back on the form or yourself. Adjust the shoulder seams to fit, and pin.

4 Stitch along the pin lines at each new shoulder seam, starting at the neckline, removing the pins as you sew.

5 Pin along the sleeve seams to make the sleeves narrower—you'll probably need to put your arm through one sleeve to figure out how much to pin.

6 Stitch along the pin line on each sleeve, removing the pins as you sew.

7 Try on the shirt and sleeves to make sure they fit. Trim the excess fabric from the new seams, leaving a ½″ seam allowance.

8 Trim the shoulder seam off the sleeves. Shorten the sleeve to your desired length plus ½″ for a seam allowance. Set aside the cut-off pieces for later.

9 Mark the center of the top edge of each sleeve with a pin. With right sides together, pin the sleeves back into the armholes, matching the underarm seams with the side seams and the center pins with the shoulder seams.

10 Sew the sleeves to the shirt with a ½″ seam allowance.

11 Lay the shirt on a flat surface as shown. From the top of each sleeve, cut a 2½″-long slit through both layers a scant ½″ away from the new armhole seam. You will end up with a 5″ opening.

12 If the armhole seam shows after you cut the shoulder slit, you may want to trim the seam from each opening.

13 Try the shirt on again to see if you want to shorten the sleeves more now that the shirt has open shoulders.

14 To make the centers of the bows, neatly cut off the hemmed bottom of the extra sleeve material. Cut 2 strips, each 3″ long, from the hems.

15 Wrap a 3″ strip, right side out, around each sleeve through the shoulder opening to the bottom and back out to the right side of the sleeve.

16 Overlap the ends and pull until you have created your desired bow by pinching the sleeve material in at the center with the strip. Hand stitch in place on the inside of the sleeve.

17 If you want to change the neckline, cut off the trim.

18 Fold the raw edge over to the wrong side in the desired shape. Pin and sew a new neckline, and cut away any excess.

Now the T-shirt fits better and has more personality, and it's fun to wear.

My New Floral Dress

Refashion Techniques

→ Shorten a skirt

→ Remove a collar from a shirt and add bias tape to finish a neckline edge

→ Add a decorative, wide elastic waistband to the exterior of a dress

→ Attach a skirt and bodice to an elastic waistband

→ Shorten a shirt

→ Shorten sleeves and finish the edges

OK, so I don't own a fashion house and I don't even sell my designs, but if I did, I would definitely have a floral line. It's so much fun to combine florals and stripes. That combo can really update a tired old unflattering dress, and it helps to give florals a bit more sophistication. It's even better when both garments are made from knits. Jackpot! No seam finishing needed. These two garments won't fray when I cut them. I love it when that happens. It makes for a quick and easy project.

1 Measure from your waistline to the length you'd like your skirt to be (see Measuring for Fit, page 20). Add ½″ for a seam allowance. Use a tape measure and a washable marking pen to mark this distance, from the hem up, all around the dress. Cut along this line. This will become the skirt of your dress. Set this aside for later.

2 Use your shoulder-to-waist measurement (see Measuring for Fit, page 20) to measure and mark the new waistline of your shirt with a washable marking pen. Add ½″ for a seam allowance. Cut off the bottom of the shirt using the line as a guide.

3 Put the shirt on your dress form and pull the collar up and away from the neckline. If you don't have a dress form, you can put it on yourself and have a trustworthy friend help you do the next step.

4 Starting at the front of the shirt, cut off the collar (and the shirt as needed) to create your desired new neckline. Stop cutting when you reach the center back, fold the cut section over on itself, and line it up. To make the other side symmetrical, cut by following along the folded-over cut edge.

5 Attach bias tape to the new neckline to keep it from stretching and to finish the edges neatly (see Bias Tape, page 29).

6 Baste around the bottom of the shirt with the longest stitch on your machine. Pull the bobbin thread to gather the shirt to your waist size.

7 Repeat Step 6 to baste around the raw edge on the top of the skirt.

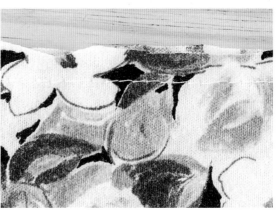

8 Cut a piece of 2″-wide knit elastic, the same size as your waist plus ½″. Overlap the ends by ½″ and sew several rows of zigzag stitches to connect the ends of the elastic. Use matching thread because your stitches will be seen at the center back of the waistband.

9 Fold the elastic waistband in quarters and mark the center front, the center back, and both sides with chalk or a pin. Repeat to mark the top of the skirt in quarters as well.

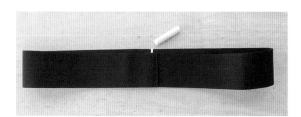

10 Pull the bobbin thread of the basting stitch to gather the skirt to your waist size. Pin the right side of the top of the skirt to the wrong side of the bottom of the elastic, overlapping them by ½″ and matching the sides, center front, and center back.

⑪ Use a zigzag stitch to attach the skirt to the elastic.

⑫ Pin the right side of the shirt to the wrong side of the elastic, overlapping them by ½″, and use a zigzag stitch to attach.

⑬ Mark the desired new length on the sleeves, adding ½″ for a seam allowance if desired. Cut the excess off the sleeves. You can leave the edges unfinished if you like or you can fold under ½″ to the wrong side and topstitch for a more finished look.

Much more modern and flattering now.

Emerald Petals Dress

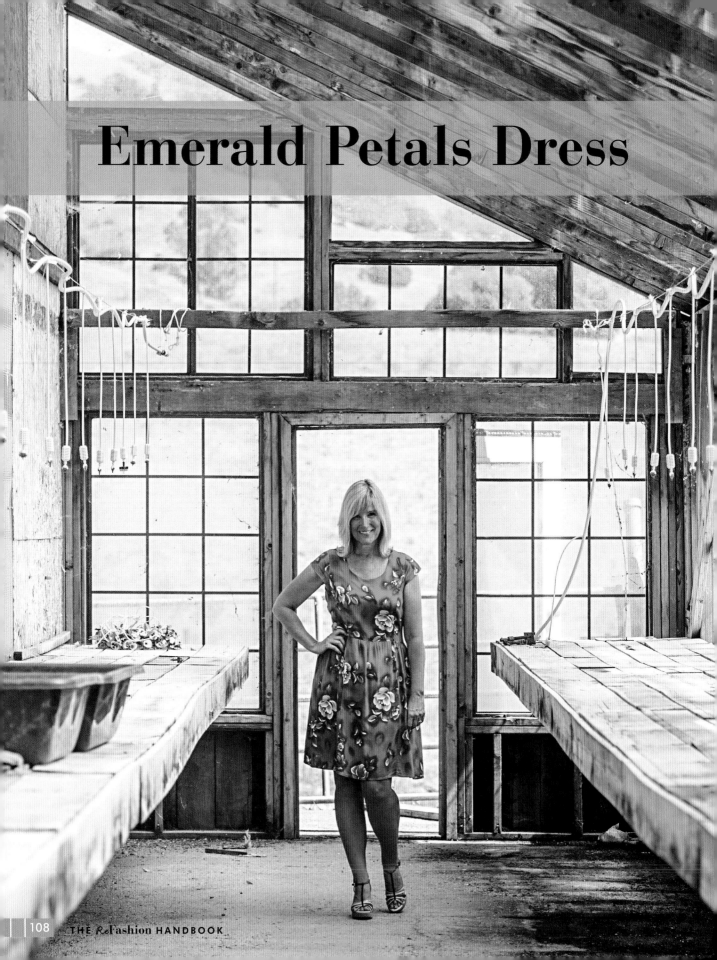

What You Will Do

Add a waist seam to change the silhouette of a dress, shorten it, and add sleeves

Refashion Techniques

→ Remove the middle section of a dress

→ Remove and reinstall a zipper

→ Reattach a bodice to a skirt

→ Make cap sleeves

Sometimes I get strange looks in the thrift stores. But I can't help it. I squeal when I come across something particularly nice with loads of promise. I know when this book comes out it will be 2014, but the Pantone color of the year 2013 is Emerald and I *love* that color. When I spied this outdated dress, I did it again. I squealed.

1 Measure yourself (or have a friend help) to determine your desired hem length (see Measuring for Fit, page 20). Add ½″ for a seam allowance and mark this distance, from the bottom up, all across the dress. Cut off the bottom of the dress—this will become the new skirt portion of your dress. If your cut line is marked across a zipper, use your seam ripper to remove the zipper from the lower section of the dress before cutting.

2 Measure the distance from your shoulder to your waist. Add ½″ for a seam allowance, mark this distance all around the bodice of the dress, and cut the new waistline, again unstitching the zipper so you don't cut through it. Set the middle piece aside to make sleeves later.

3 Measure your zipper. Using your seam ripper, open the center back seam of the skirt piece to fit the length of the zipper.

4 Put your machine on the longest stitch and baste along the top of the skirt to create a gathering stitch.

5 Pull the bobbin thread to gather the skirt material to fit the bodice.

6 Mark the bottom edge of the bodice in quarters (center front, center back, and 2 sides). Mark the top of the skirt in quarters as well. With right sides together, pin the top of the skirt to the bottom of the bodice. Ease the skirt gathers as needed to match the side seams, center front, and center back.

7 Sew the bottom of the bodice to the top of the skirt with a ½″ seam allowance.

8 Reinstall the back zipper (see Installing a Centered Zipper, page 34).

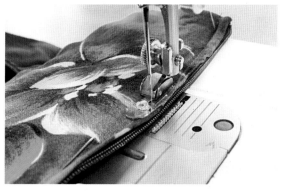

9 Add cap sleeves made from the middle section of the dress if you desire (see Making Cap Sleeves, page 39).

I **love** my new dress and I sure hope the color emerald stays current for a few more years. I'll have to try very hard not to squeal with joy each time I put this dress on.

Leather Laptop Sleeve

Refashion Techniques

→ Customize the size and shape of a case

→ Sew leather

→ Finish the edges of leather

→ Make a button loop closure

I hope you don't shy away from the possibilities of old leather jackets and coats. My thrift store seems to have a limitless supply of them. Once in a while I hear them call out to me with a slow, deep, cowboy drawl. Sometimes it's a sophisticated English voice, but no matter what the accent, or where they came from, they always say the same thing: "Take me home. Make me special again." You don't need to fear sewing with leather or suede. You can sew just about any leather with a regular sewing machine and a size 110/18 leather needle.

This soft black leather came from the back of an old stained leather jacket. Let's make it special by turning it into a leather laptop sleeve.

You will need leather, some fun fabric for the lining, stiff but lightweight fusible interfacing (I used Pellon 808 Craft-Fuse), spray adhesive, a large button, and some embroidery thread.

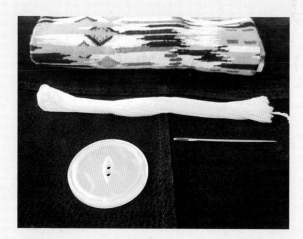

1 Flatten out into a smooth, single layer whatever garment you are using to make your case. Place your laptop on the leather and fold it over to determine what size to cut the leather. Add ½″ on each side for a seam allowance and to allow for the thickness of the laptop. I have a 13″ laptop, and I cut my leather 14¼″ × 19″. To get a nice straight line, use your rotary cutter and a ruler to cut the leather.

2 Cut a piece of lining fabric and a piece of interfacing the same size as the cut piece of leather.

3 Following the manufacturer's instructions, fuse the interfacing to the wrong side of the lining fabric.

4 Again following the manufacturer's instructions, use spray adhesive to adhere the interfaced side of the lining to the wrong side of the leather.

5 Use embroidery thread and a large needle to sew a blanket stitch on what will be the open edges of the case (see Blanket Stitch, page 26). You can also try using a glover's needle, which has a triangular tip that pierces the leather easily. Remember that any holes you make will remain, unlike with fabric.

6 Sew a button, centered from side to side, about 2½″ down from a blanket-stitched edge. Use a regular hand-sewing needle and strong thread.

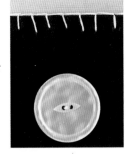

7 Fold the leather in half with the lining sides together, matching up blanket-stitched edges. Sew along each side with a 110/18 leather needle, leaving a ¼″ seam allowance. Trim the sides if you need to, because sometimes leather has slight differences in thickness and may stretch as you sew.

8 Slip the laptop in the case to check the fit. Measure from the center of the button over the open edge and about 5″ down the other side. Double this number and cut a strip ¼″ wide by this length from the remaining leather for the button loop. Then cut a triangle with sides about 1½″ from the same leather.

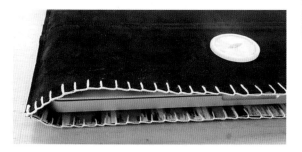

9 Fold the leather strip in half. With the laptop still in the case, slip the fold around the button and bring the strips to the other side. Place the triangular piece of leather over the ends as shown and mark the placement. Remove the laptop and stitch all around the edges of the triangle, making sure to catch the ends of the button loop in more than one place.

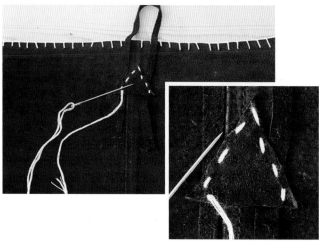

Slide your laptop inside, slip the loop over the button, and off you go with a chic new leather laptop sleeve.

Renegade Ikat Bag

Finished size: 12″ wide × 13½″ high × 3″ deep

What You Will Do

Make a bag from secondhand materials

Refashion Techniques

→ Make boxed corners to add dimension

→ Sew leather

"I think I have too much fabric. I don't think I should buy any more fabric. I don't want to go fabric shopping." Those are things you'll hear me say . . . *never*! I'm of the belief that there is no such thing as too much fabric. I know I'm not alone in this type of worship. You know who you are. I don't need to mention any names. But you know, your fabric doesn't always have to come new from a fabric store. I had been looking for some ikat fabric unsuccessfully for quite some time when this tablecloth whistled at me across the sweaters from the linen section at the Goodwill store. I went over to see what it wanted. And before I knew it, it had hijacked my cart and wouldn't get out. It forced me to take it home. Really, Steve, that's exactly how it happened.

As soon as we returned home, I searched through my stash and found just the right treasures to combine with this pushy tablecloth to make it into a new bag. The black leather sleeve was left over from the laptop bag project (see Leather Laptop Sleeve, page 112). The place mats have been on and off my tables for more than fifteen years. The black leather belt successfully seduced me at my local thrift shop one sunny afternoon and ended up coming home with me. (Belts do that, you know.) And the denim pocket was also left over from a previous project.

You will need fabric for the outside of the bag, leather for the base of the bag, place mats or other material for lining, a leather belt for the strap, a repurposed pocket, and fusible interfacing (I used Pellon 808 Craft-Fuse).

Cutting

→ Cut 2 rectangles 13″ × 16″ each from outer fabric, lining, and interfacing.

→ Cut 2 rectangles 13″ × 6″ each from leather for the bag base.

1 Follow the manufacturer's instructions to fuse the interfacing to the wrong side of each outer fabric piece.

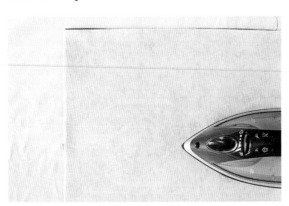

2 Place a 13″ × 6″ leather piece on top of a 13″ × 16″ outer fabric piece, both right sides up, aligning them at the bottom edges. Pin and stitch together along the bottom 13″ edge with a ½″ seam allowance. Use a 110/18 leather needle in your machine. Repeat this step with the remaining leather and outer bag pieces.

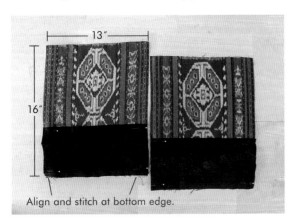

Align and stitch at bottom edge.

3 Topstitch (page 25) across the top of each leather piece ¼″ from the edge.

Topstitch here.

④ With right sides together, pin and sew the layered leather / outer bag pieces together along the sides and the bottom with a ½″ seam allowance.

⑤ Pinch each bottom corner together, aligning the side and bottom seams, and sew diagonally across the corners 1½″ in from the points.

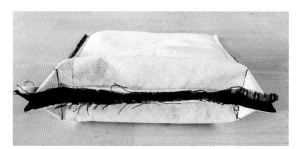

⑥ Trim the excess ½″ away from the corner seams. Now you have boxed corners.

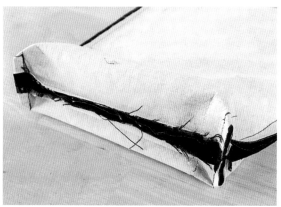

⑦ Find a pocket that will fit inside your new bag. Cut out the pocket very close to the seam.

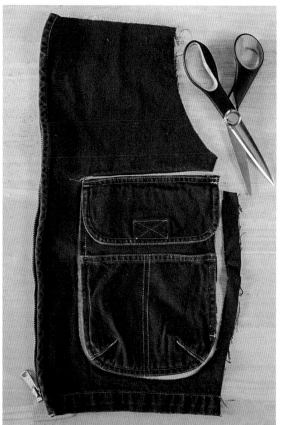

8 Pin the pocket, centered, onto the right side of one of the lining pieces.

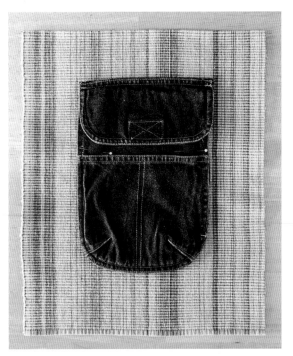

9 Use the 100/18 leather needle or a heavy-duty denim needle to stitch the pocket onto the lining piece, following along an existing stitching line.

10 Repeat Steps 4–6 to sew the lining pieces together, leaving a 7″ section open in the bottom, and box the corners.

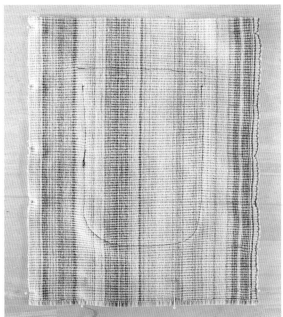

⓫ Making sure to use the leather needle, stitch the ends of the belt 1″ down from the top on the side seams on the outer bag. Stitch a square the width of the belt, and then stitch across the square diagonally in both directions for a secure hold.

⓬ Pull the belt down so it is out of the way.

⓭ With right sides together, place the outer bag inside the lining.

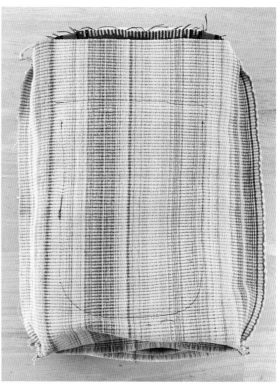

⓮ Line up the raw edges and side seams, and pin around the top edges of the bag.

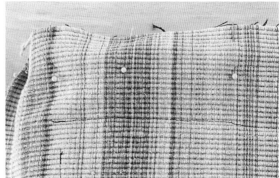

15 Stitch the top edges together with a ½″ seam.

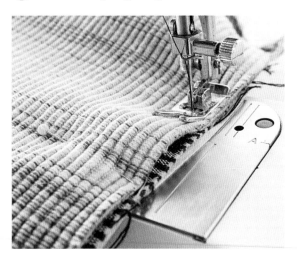

16 Turn the bag right side out by reaching up into the opening you left in the bottom of the lining to pull out the rest of the bag.

17 Stitch the bottom of the lining closed using a whipstitch (see Whipstitch, page 26).

18 Push the lining back into the bag. Press around the upper edge.

Now the tablecloth is happily enjoying its new life as a bag. However, I am starting to hear some muffled sounds coming from the blue fabric drawer. I think the rest of the tablecloth is starting to beg me to make it into a dress. Maybe I should just keep the drawer closed for a while.

Cowgirl Clutch

Refashion Techniques

→ Sew with a zipper foot

→ Use a belt closure

Quite often refashioning is quick and painless. I found this set of 3 place mats at Goodwill for half price, making them only 35 cents for all 3. You can make a simple clutch from a place mat in just a few minutes.

1 If your place mat has fringe, trim it off of 1 short side.

2 Fold the place mat into thirds, with the fringed edge folded on top. Then flip the top edge up and away, and pin the place mat together at the sides through 2 layers.

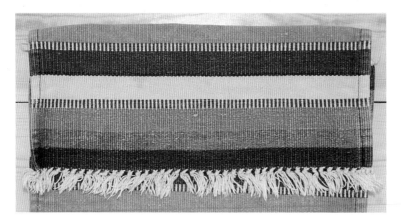

3 Change to a zipper foot, and if you'd like to add an interesting detail you could use 2 different colors for the top and bottom threads.

4 Stitch the side seams as close to the finished edge as possible.

5 Fold over the top, wrap it with a fun belt, and you've got a great clutch to use with jeans.

About the Author

Beth Huntington is founder and designer of The Renegade Seamstress, a blog known for its simple, stylish, and straightforward refashion photo tutorials. She wants to inspire even the most inexperienced sewists to try this environmentally friendly and economical way to transform thrift store finds into fashionable pieces of clothing that can be worn anywhere.

When she's not sewing or refashioning, she spends her days in a sunlit classroom full of energetic and enthusiastic kindergarteners. When she's not teaching, you might find her skiing down a mountain, wakeboarding the river, or growing pumpkins and daisies and collecting eggs at her Oregon home with her family, two dogs, and six chickens.

You can visit her at The Renegade Seamstress, chicenvelopements.wordpress.com.

stash BOOKS ®

fabric arts for a handmade lifestyle

If you're craving beautiful authenticity in a time of mass-production...Stash Books is for you. Stash Books is a line of how-to books celebrating fabric arts for a handmade lifestyle. Backed by C&T Publishing's solid reputation for quality, Stash Books will inspire you with contemporary designs, clear and simple instructions, and engaging photography.